A LIVE * LEARN * SHARE: EARTH-1

In the Night Sky

The Astrological Zodiac for Children

Rayne Storm

Dedication

For my Sweet and Wonderful boys
True blessings who are as heavenly as
Day and Night!

To Evelien and her family
Thank you for your friendship,
our sisterly chats and
ALL of your helpful advice!
knuffels

And to Michael... for his continued support with
my many endeavors!

To the Earth-based Spiritual Families... For
whom this book was created for,
May you always remember the Deities..., May
you always want to learn more...
And may you always remain grounded as you
walk along your Earthen path!
Blessed Be!

Acknowledgements

To Lora... You're my inspiration
to do more for children *hugs*
Thank you for your friendship,
encouragement... and for Pooka Pages
(www.pookapages.com).

To Lisa... with Editor's Cove
(www.editorscove.com) ...
Thank you so much for your helpful and
meticulous editing skills.

To Laura...... Thank you for your assistance
with some celestial nuisances.

To Schiffer Publishing... Thank you for the
opportunity to make this happen.

And, to my Magickal Library... May you
NEVER stop growing!

Copyright © 2013 by Rayne Storm
Library of Congress Control Number: 2013955259

All rights reserved. No part of this work may be reproduced or used in any form or by any means—graphic, electronic, or mechanical, including photocopying or information storage and retrieval systems—without written permission from the publisher.
The scanning, uploading and distribution of this book or any part thereof via the Internet or via any other means without the permission of the publisher is illegal and punishable by law. Please purchase only authorized editions and do not participate in or encourage the electronic piracy of copyrighted materials.
"Schiffer," "Schiffer Publishing, Ltd. & Design," and the "Design of pen and inkwell" are registered trademarks of Schiffer Publishing, Ltd.

Schiffer Books are available at special discounts for bulk purchases for sales promotions or premiums. Special editions, including personalized covers, corporate imprints, and excerpts can be created in large quantities for special needs. For more information contact the publisher:

Published by Schiffer Publishing, Ltd.
4880 Lower Valley Road
Atglen, PA 19310
Phone: (610) 593-1777; Fax: (610) 593-2002
E-mail: Info@schifferbooks.com.

For the largest selection of fine reference books on this and related subjects, please visit our website at **www.schifferbooks.com**. We are always looking for people to write books on new and related subjects. If you have an idea for a book, please contact us at

THE ZODIAC SIGNS ...10

Aries ...13

Taurus ...19

Gemini ...25

Cancer ...31

Leo ...37

Virgo ...43

Libra ...49

Scorpio ...55

Sagittarius ...61

Capricorn ...67

Aquarius ...73

Pisces ...79

THE THIRTEENTH ZODIAC: OPHIUCHUS ...85

ANSWER KEYS ...88

Author' Note:

Please understand that this book is not an exact science of the stars. Images are only meant to show proximity of their placement in the sky. As with many things, dates, interpretations, and illustrations may vary. Some constellations may appear different than you are accustomed to seeing them, but the meanings and representations are still the same or similar. Some stories have been purposefully changed or altered, to make them more age appropriate.

This book is only meant to be a guide to a child's understanding of constellations, in particular the Zodiac/Sun Signs. It covers the basics and is meant to be a beginner's guide to discovering the aspects of the Astrological Zodiac and an introduction to some of the stories that accompany each Zodiac sign.

BASICS

Polaris the Center Point...

Polaris, or the North Star as it's more commonly known, is the most recognizable star in the night sky, and it's the only one that does not move.

Actually, none of the stars move. As the Earth moves in a circular pattern, the stars seem to move in the heavenly sky. The North Star, of all the stars seems to stand still only because it is directly over the northern-most point of the Earth.

Finding Polaris...

If you can find Polaris, you can navigate your way at night without a compass. The reason you can do this is because Polaris always points north. So, if you need to travel north, you should walk towards Polaris; if you need to travel south, it should seem like Polaris is following you. Knowing where Polaris is can also help you locate the Astrological Zodiac constellations in the sky.

CHALLENGE: Do you know how to use a compass?
Can you find north and locate Polaris?
Which constellation uses the north star as its tail?

Answer: Little Bear/Ursa Minor

What is the Astrological Zodiac?

The Astrological Zodiac is also referred to as the Sun Signs in astrology. The Sun Signs change with the agricultural seasons or the position of the Sun in its relation to the Earth during different times of the year.

These Sun Signs are a group of 12 constellations that are known to have influences on our individual characteristics, depending on the Sun Sign under which each of us were born.

The 12 ASTROLOGICAL ZODIACS in order are:

ARIES	LIBRA
TAURUS	SCORPIO
GEMINI	SAGITTARIUS
CANCER	CAPRICORN
LEO	AQUARIUS
VIRGO	PISCES

What are Constellations?

Constellations are groupings of stars. They aren't just any group of stars. They are specific groupings of stars that people, astronomers, scientists, or anyone can use to help guide them when the sun goes down. They circle around us in the heavens, as the Earth makes its way around the Sun every year.

ASPECT CHART:

Zodiac and Dates	Symbol	Element	Celestial Body	Mode
ARIES Mar. 21 - Apr. 19	♈	▲ FIRE	♂ MARS	Cardinal
TAURUS Apr. 20 - May 20	♉	▽ EARTH	♀ VENUS	Fixed
GEMINI May 21 - June 20	♊	▲ AIR	☿ MERCURY	Mutable
CANCER June 21 - July 22	♋	▽ WATER	☾ MOON	Cardinal
LEO July 23 - Aug. 22	♌	▲ FIRE	☉ SUN	Fixed
VIRGO Aug. 23 - Oct. 22	♍	▽ EARTH	☿ MERCURY	Mutable
LIBRA Sept. 23 - Oct. 22	♎	▲ AIR	♀ VENUS	Cardinal
SCORPIO Oct. 23 - Nov. 21	♏	▽ WATER	♇ PLUTO	Fixed
SAGITTARIUS Nov. 22 - Dec. 21	♐	▲ FIRE	♃ JUPITER	Mutable
CAPRICORN Dec. 22 - Jan. 19	♑	▽ EARTH	♄ SATURN	Cardinal
AQUARIUS Jan. 20 - Feb. 18	♒	▲ AIR	♅ URANUS	Fixed
PISCES Feb. 19 - Mar. 20	♓	▽ WATER	♆ NEPTUNE	Mutable

Each Zodiac has its own set of trait characteristics. In addition to each Zodiac having their own symbol, they are also assigned (among other things) an Element, a Celestial Body, and a Mode.

HOW TO FIND YOUR ZODIAC SIGN

Match your date of birth to the Zodiac that holds that same date. For example, if you were born on October 1st, then you would be a Libra

THE ELEMENTS

Each of the four Elements has been assigned to a specific Zodiac, and each Element brings with it its own characteristics:

FIRE

the Spirit/Unpredictable

Zodiacs with a FIRE Element are lively and bright, outgoing and active, dynamic and impulsive. They trust in their instincts, and they should, since they are very passionate and adventurous individuals.

Aries
Leo
Sagittarius

EARTH

the Body/Action Oriented

Zodiacs with an EARTH Element are grounded and controlled, practical and straight forward, stable and structured. They tend to be concerned with what's on the surface, and they are dependable and headstrong.

Taurus
Virgo
Capricorn

AIR

the Mind/Unpredictable

Zodiacs with an AIR Element are intellectual and logical, social and communicative, creative and expressive. They can be out of touch with reality and with their thinking because they are very elusive and eccentric.

Gemini
Libra
Aquarius

WATER

the Emotions/Complex

Zodiacs with a WATER Element are nurturing and sensitive, in-tune and flowing, receptive and responsive. They have an ability to deal with others, and they become deeply involved and have empathic qualities.

Cancer
Scorpio
Pisces

CHALLENGE:
Which Element influences your Zodiac? Do you think that it's accurate in relation to how you are, how you behave, and how you interact with the world and with others? Why do you think that is so? Which element do you believe fits you best?

CELESTIAL BODIES

Just as each Zodiac is influenced by individual Elements, they are also influenced by Celestial Bodies, also known as Planetary Influences.

SUN ☉	Masculine Energy/Active Energies A Star of Individual Self/Ego, Giver of Life Person of strength and leadership, has a will and a desire to succeed, contains a creative spark	Zodiac: **LEO**
MERCURY ☿	Neutral Energy/Restless Energies Planet of Reason and Opportunity Person of self-expression, quick acting, adaptable, witty, objective, opinionated, and intellectual	Zodiac: **GEMINI** **VIRGO**
VENUS ♀	Feminine Energy/Harmonious Energies Planet of Love and of Money Person of love and pleasure, teaches sensitivity and understanding, exudes joy, enhances elegance and beauty	Zodiac: **TAURUS** **LIBRA**
MOON ☾	Feminine Energy/Emotional Energies Moon of Inner Energy, Inner Being Person of matter and personality, in touch with their emotions, experiencing an up-and-down journey	Zodiac: **CANCER**
MARS ♂	Masculine Energy/Dynamic Energies Planet of Passion and Fiery Energy Person of action, highly competitive, assertive, extremely ambitious, courageous and fearless	Zodiac: **ARIES**
JUPITER ♃	Masculine Energy/Exploration Energies Planet of Higher Education and Thinking Person of luck, growth and well-being, spirituality and psychic awareness, goes the distance to find answers and explores things on all levels	Zodiac: **SAGITTARIUS**

SATURN ♄

Masculine Energy/Teaching Energies
Planet of Karma, Responsibility and Acceptance
Person of tasks/taskmaster, commanding to work and work hard to be successful, acknowledges limits and plans for the future

Zodiac: **CAPRICORN**

URANUS

Neutral Energy/Profound Energies
Planet of Rebellion
Person of new thoughts and ideas, non-traditional, always looking for something new, independent, erratic with unusual behaviors

Zodiac: **AQUARIUS**

NEPTUNE ♆

Feminine Energy/Enchanted Energies
Planet of Illusion and all that is Mysterious
Person of glamour and flattery, influences dreams and sleep, individuals are affected based on how the energy is accepted and used

Zodiac: **PISCES**

PLUTO ♇

Masculine Energy/Stimulates Energies
Planet of Transformation and Rebirth
Person of obsession and power, rules all that is hidden and secret, goes within to the subconscious to find treasure

Zodiac: **SCORPIO**

CHALLENGE:

Which Celestial Body influences your Zodiac?
Do have the traits, as described by the Celestial Body for your Sun Sign?
How do you think you are similar?
How are you different?
Why do you think that is?

THE MODES

There are three forces, or modes, that can influence the way an individual interacts with the world. One mode is assigned to each of the Zodiacs.

CARDINAL
Intricate/Goal-Oriented

For each Zodiac sign that contains the Cardinal aspect, there is an elemental quality that determines how they present themselves in their particular style.

ARIES with the Element of Fire: dynamic

CANCER with the Element of Water: goes with the flow

LIBRA with the Element of Air: creative

CAPRICORN with the Element of Earth: grounded

FIXED
Loyal/Stable

An individual with a Fixed Mode aspect for their Zodiac Sign is respected for their sense of purpose. They plant themselves firmly to achieve something solid, and can be very stubborn when it comes to change.

TAURUS

LEO

SCORPIO

AQUARIUS

MUTABLE
Adaptable/Flexible

An individual with a Mutable sign is adaptable and very flexible. They have a little bit of chaos in their lives because they can view life from many perspectives.

GEMINI

VIRGO

SAGITTARIUS

PISCES

Do you see what I see?
Take a closer look with me...
For hidden amongst the stars so high,
Are stories illustrated in the sky!
Stories with lessons that unfold,
Continually passed down and retold.
Guiding us with their heavenly projection...
Pointing us in the right direction,
Marking points along the frontier...
During each agricultural year!

THE ZODIAC SIGNS

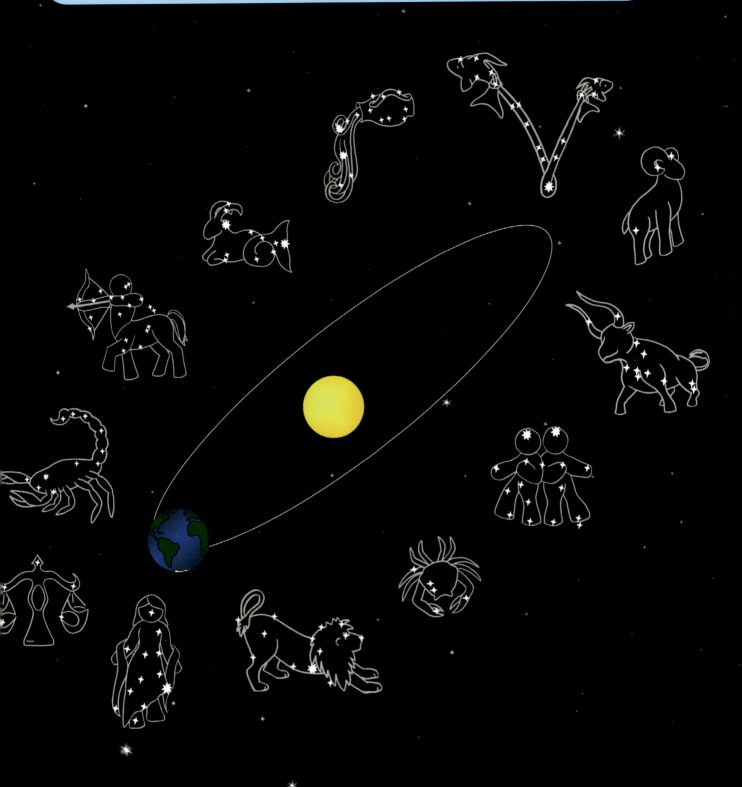

Do you see what I see? Who or what...might it be?
What teachings could be held so high...
As to be written in the night sky?

ARIES

13

March 21 — April 19

ARIES
the Ram

I am Aries. Aries, the Ram
Known for my bruteness,
And for being daring and brash
I am the Leader of the Zodiac!
From time to time, I can be a bit pushy
But that's just to keep them all in line.
I stand majestically
As my presence commands
I am as quick-witted as I am gullible,
Approaching life committed...
My motto is, "I Do!"

DID YOU KNOW?

Aries marks the point at which the sun meets the Vernal Equinox. Equinox means the point at which day and night are equal. Vernal implies that it occurs in the Spring. The Autumnal Equinox occurs in the fall.

ARIES, the Ram
March 21 - April 19

The first of the twelve constellations, Aries is positioned between Taurus, the Bull, and Pisces, the Fish.

The Aries star cluster is said to be one of the oldest of all constellations, dating back to the time of the Ancient Babylonians, Egyptians and Greeks.

Aries is also located in the middle of a triangle, with its sides being Cetus (the sea monster), Perseus (the hero) and Andromeda (the chained princess).

Aries was sacred because of his golden fleece, which was said to have the great power of immortality, returning life to those who had died.

Born under Aries

You are said to be...

- Gifted, Daring, and Quick-Witted

But you can also be...

- Gullible, Brash, and Pushy

Colors: RED, WHITE
Stone: DIAMOND
Mode: CARDINAL
Metal: IRON
Body Part: the HEAD

Fill in the missing blank *-OR-* Draw in the missing symbol. (See Aspect Chart on **page 5**.)

Symbol: ARIES   Element: FIRE

Aries represents the motto, "I DO"
★ To DO: to be a leader and get things done
★ To DO: to perform tasks under pressure
★ To DO: to inspire others around you to carry out plans

If you are ...
★ Unable to complete projects due to focus
★ Lacking a direction or feeling like you are in a cloud
★ Finding yourself in conflicts and arguments

Then, Aries teaches you to...
★ Find what it is you want, and then make it happen
★ Search your soul deeply to resolve unsolved issues
★ Learn to listen more, speak less, or not speak at all

Points towards the Pisces Constellation

★ Using the two stars in the horns of Aries, you can point yourself in the direction of Pisces.

★ Aries, doesn't have any bright stars and is a very small constellation

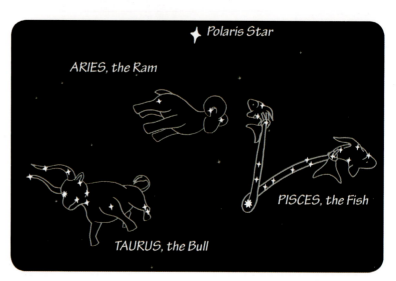

Using the words listed below, find the words associated with Aries in the puzzle. Words are horizontal, vertical and diagonal.

ARIES	MARS	HEAD	RUBY	BRASH	GULLIBLE	QUICK WITTED	I DO
RAM	FIRE	PINK	OLDEST	PUSHY	CARDINAL	VERNAL EQUINOX	
FIRST	IRON	WHITE	DARING	GIFTED	IMMORTALITY	GOLDEN FLEECE	

Do you see what I see? Who or what...might it be?
What teachings could be held so high...
As to be written in the night sky?

TAURUS

April 20 — May 20

TAURUS
the bull

I am Taurus. Taurus, the Bull

I am a reliable and loyal friend.

It is unwise to rush me

While I take time to think and ponder.

To defend and to protect, that is my job

Standing as guard over the Seven Pleiades Sisters

With confidence I stare down Orion.

I am the epitome of endurance and persistence.

I am as determined as I am stubborn…

Approaching life sensibly…

My motto is, "I Have!"

DID YOU KNOW?

Bulls, like Taurus, are color blind. It is not the vibrant red color of the flag used to draw in a bull's attention; it is the flapping movement of the flag that encourages the animal to charge and to advance towards the flag.

TAURUS, the Bull
April 20 - May 20

The second of the twelve constellations, Taurus is positioned between Aries, the Ram, and Gemini, the Twins.

Orion, the hunter, once pursued the seven daughters of Atlas. But Atlas had been forced to carry the load of the world on his shoulders, so he pleaded for their protection. Zeus turned them into heavenly stars and placed them in the sky to be protected by Taurus. As Taurus moves across the sky, the rainy season is said to begin. It is thought that the daughters of Atlas, mourning their father's impossible task, cry tears in the form of rain.

Born under Taurus

You are said to be...

- Loyal, Strong, and Determined

But you can also be...

- Jealous, Stubborn, and Head-Strong

Colors: YELLOW, RED
Stone: WHITE SAPPHIRE
Mode: FIXED
Metal: COPPER
Body Part: NECK and SHOULDERS

Fill in the missing blank **-OR-** Draw in the missing symbol. (See Aspect Chart on **page 5**.)

Symbol: TAURUS   Celestial: VENUS

Taurus represents the motto, "I OWN"
★ To OWN: to possess the endurance to go forward
★ To OWN: to possess a value of trust, a dependability
★ To OWN: to possess persistence and stand your ground

If you are...
★ Out of touch with the world around you and its beauty
★ Disgusted and dissatisfied with most everything
★ Feeling as though you can't trust anyone or anything

Then Taurus teaches us to...
★ Realize that you need to be positive, so you can receive positive
★ Seek out your Spirituality and build/re-build your Faith
★ Take control of your life and discover your inner harmony

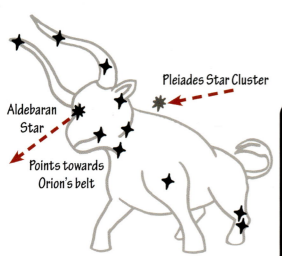

- ★ The Taurus constellation contains the Aldebaran Star. Aldebaran means "follower" in Arabic.
- ★ The Aldebaran Star follows the Pleiades Star Cluster across the sky. The Pleiades Star Cluster represents the seven daughters of Atlas.

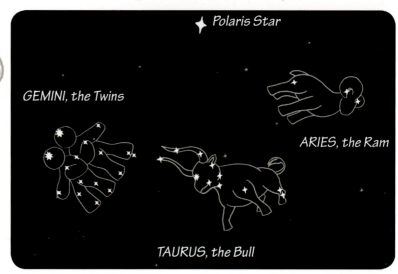

Solve the math equations. Then match the answer to the letter. Decode the names of the Seven Sisters of the Pleiades Star Cluster.

12 - 4 = ___ = A   10 + 3 = ___ = I   3 - 3 = ___ = O   5 + 5 = ___ = T

1 + 0 = ___ = C   10 - 7 = ___ = L   8 - 6 = ___ = P   4 + 8 = ___ = Y

2 + 3 = ___ = E   13 - 2 = ___ = M   9 - 5 = ___ = R   12 + 12 = ___ = Z

7 - 1 = ___ = G   15 - 6 = ___ = N   3 + 4 = ___ = S

1 __ __ __ __ __ __ __ __
   8 7 10 5 4 0 2 5

2 __ __ __ __ __ __ __
   10 8 12 6 5 10 8

3 __ __ __ __
   11 8 13 8

4 __ __ __ __ __ __
    1 5 3 8 5 9 0

5 __ __ __ __ __ __ __
    5 3 5 1 10 4 8

6 __ __ __ __ __
   11 5 4 0 2 5

7 __ __ __ __ __ __
    8 3 1 12 0 9 5

Do you see what I see? Who or what...might it be?
What teachings could be held so high...
As to be written in the night sky?

GEMINI

May 21 — June 21

GEMINI
the twins

We are Gemini. Gemini, the Twins.

Our story is known across many an ocean and sea.

I am Pollux, I am strength, and I am immortal.

I am Castor, I am skill, and unlike my brother,

I am a mortal.

But, with our differences aside

We are revered for our Brotherly Love...

We are funny and we can be very talkative, too,

Always on the go, we never care to be tied down.

We have an insatiable curiosity for life,

As we approach life ingeniously...

Our motto is, "I Think!"

DID YOU KNOW?

Twins can actually be born on different days, in different years, and even during different millenniums. Very Rare, but it's possible...IF one was born on December 31, 1999—just before midnight—and the other was born January 1, 2000—just after midnight!

GEMINI, the Twins

May 21 - June 21

The third of the twelve constellations, Gemini is positioned between Taurus, the Bull, and Cancer, the Crab. Gemini represents the twins, Castor and Pollux.

The twin brothers are sons to Leda, but have different fathers. Pollux was the son of Jupiter, the King of Gods, and Castor was the son of Tyndareus, the King of Sparta. Their sister was Helen of Troy.

Growing up, Castor and Pollux were the best of friends. Never argumentative, they would always consult each other. They were inseparable!

Mariners often regarded the twins as the protectors of sailors and of sailing ships.

Born under Gemini

You are said to be...

- Talkative, Curious, and Funny

But you can also be...

- Annoying, Tense, and Gossipy

Colors: GREEN, GOLD
Stone: EMERALD
Mode: MUTABLE
Metal: QUICK-SILVER
Body Part: ARMS and HANDS

Fill in the missing blank -OR- Draw in the missing symbol. (See Aspect Chart on page 5.)

Symbol: GEMINI

Gemini represents the motto, "I THINK"
★ To THINK: to be adaptable to anything
★ To THINK: to communicate clearly
★ To THINK: to be inquisitive, to question

If you are...
★ Superficial, only presenting the outer you to others
★ Creating problems to cease the quietness
★ Finding mischievousness due to boredom

Then Gemini teaches you...
★ To let others get to know the inner you, the real you
★ To put your time into productive hobbies to keep yourself busy
★ Follow through with whatever you have committed yourself to

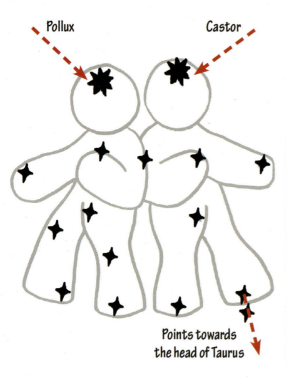

★ The Castor star is six stars, but appears to be one star. The Pollux star is an orange giant star.

★ The two stars in the foot of the Twin Castor point towards the Head of Taurus, the Bull

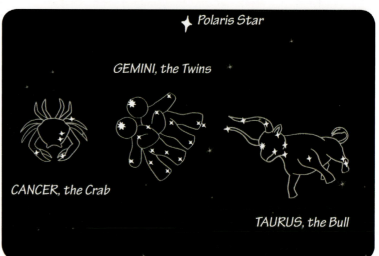

An Aspect of Gemini and the Messenger of the Gods? _____

Answer the questions below and fill in the boxes. The answer to the question in the box above, will be revealed in the circles.

1. _____, the Twins

2. Gemini Stone

3. Opposite of mortal

4. Son of Tyndareus

5. Son of Jupiter

6. Elemental aspect

7. Sister, Helen of _____

Do you see what I see? Who or what...might it be?
What teachings could be held so high...
As to be written in the night sky?

CANCER

June 21 — July 22

CANCER
the crab

I am Cancer. Cancer, the Crab

As seen by my tracks, I walk sideways

Preferring to go around problems and slipping into cracks

Unless of course, I am provoked into taking a stand.

I spend my days collecting the most fantastic things.

Hanging onto these prized possessions,

I beautify and enrich my surroundings.

And, just beyond my tough exterior and claws

Is a sensitive and caring friend

Who approaches the everyday with empathy

My motto is, "I Feel!"

DID YOU KNOW?

The reason a crab walks sideways is because their knees don't bend forward like humans. This is actually helpful because it allows them to squeeze into holes and cracks, protecting themselves from becoming a tasty snack to other animals.

CANCER, the Crab

June 21 - July 22

The fourth of the twelve constellations, Cancer is positioned between Gemini, the Twins, and Leo, the Lion.

There are a couple of stories about how Cancer came to be a constellation. One story says that, during a battle, Hera, the Queen of the Gods, sent the giant crab to aid in the battle. But, when the crab pinched Hercules' toe, Hercules crushed him. For his bravery though, Hera immortalized him in the heavens.

Another story tells how Poseidon left the giant crab to look after his daughters, the water nymphs, while he battled Typhon. When Poseidon returned, he honored the Crab with immortality.

Born under Cancer

You are said to be…

- Dependable, Friendly, and Understanding

But you can also be…

- Moody, Touchy, and Protective

Colors: GREEN, BROWN
Stone: PEARL
Mode: CARDINAL
Metal: SILVER
Body Part: CHEST

Fill in the missing blank *-OR-* Draw in the missing symbol. (See Aspect Chart on **page 5**.)

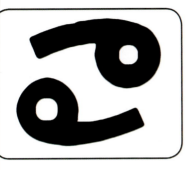

Celestial: **MOON**

Cancer represents the motto, "I FEEL"

★ To FEEL: to perceive with intuition and to trust it

★ To FEEL: to perceive with empathy and be sympathetic

★ To FEEL: to perceive a situation and go cautiously

If you are...

★ Putting things off until the last minute

★ Self-absorbed to the point you don't notice others

★ Unable to do as you are asked without getting upset

Then Cancer teaches you to...

★ Take care of things - make it a priority

★ Make it a habit of recognizing others around you

★ Follow by example, and you will get where you are going

★ Besides its faint stars, Cancer is also one of the smallest Zodiac Constellations.

★ To find the constellation, it requires a very dark sky; it looks like an upside down "Y"

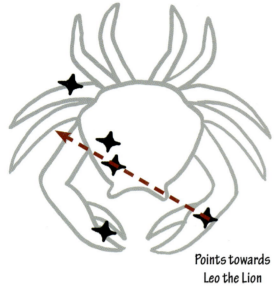

Points towards Leo the Lion

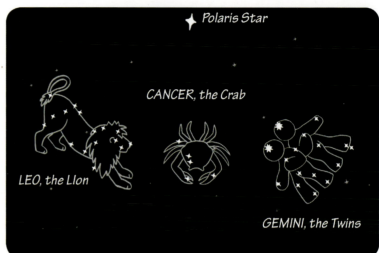

Crossword Puzzle

DOWN

1. Friendly and____

2. Walking side _____

4. Celestial body

5. Cancer's metal

6. Cancer's stone

ACROSS

3. Cancer, the _____

6. God of the Sea

7. Elemental aspect

8. Immortalized for being _____

Do you see what I see? Who or what...might it be?
What teachings could be held so high...
As to be written in the night sky?

LEO

July 23 — August 22

LEO
the lion

I am Leo. Leo, the Lion.

With great pride and a robust confidence,

I am the regal king of beasts.

There is no need for caution, no need to be afraid.

I only aspire to be the center of attention.

Determined to have consistency,

Stubbornly I resist any change.

When I see that there are no available opportunities,

I have an ability to find the easy way out.

I am as ambitious as I am enthusiastic.

Approaching life flamboyantly

My motto is, "I Will!"

DID YOU KNOW?

That lions really aren't the "Kings of the Jungle"? Lions don't even live in jungles; they prefer grasslands and plains areas. And although lions once roamed throughout Africa, Europe and Asia...today, they can only be found in the wild, in Africa and in a national park in India.

LEO, the Lion
July 23 - August 22

The fifth of the twelve constellations, Leo is positioned between Cancer, the Crab, and Virgo, the Goddess.

Many different cultures identified this particular constellation, the Regulus Star, as a Lion.

In Egypt, the lion became synonymous with this constellation because as the Regulus star crossed the sky, the lions would make their way down to the Nile river to escape the intense desert sun.

For the Egyptians, when Leo made his appearance in the night sky, they knew that the Nile River would flood the lands, preparing the soil to be sowed.

Born under Leo

You are said to be...

- Playful, Flamboyant, and Likeable

But you can also be...

- Controlling, Egotistical, and Overbearing

Colors: RED, BLACK
Stone: RUBY
Mode: FIXED
Metal: GOLD
Body Part: BACK and HEART

Fill in the missing blank *-OR-* Draw in the missing symbol. (See Aspect Chart on page 5.)

 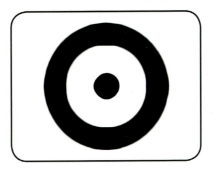 

Element: FIRE

Leo represents the motto, "I WILL"

★ To WILL: to desire a powerful and noble stature

★ To WILL: to desire a protective and loyal side

★ To WILL: to desire fun and a warm-hearted nature

If you are...

★ Your own worst enemy—when things don't go your way

★ Egotistical or have an exaggerated idea of oneself

★ Constantly striving to get the attention of others

Then Leo teaches us to...

★ Stop trying so hard and let others see the real you

★ Get your ego in check and serve a higher purpose

★ Base your expectations on what you can give, not what you want or expect

★ The Regulus Star is the brightest star in the constellation and one of the brightest in the night sky.

★ Within the lion, there is a pattern of stars seen as a backwards question mark, with the Regulus star as the Leo's beating heart.

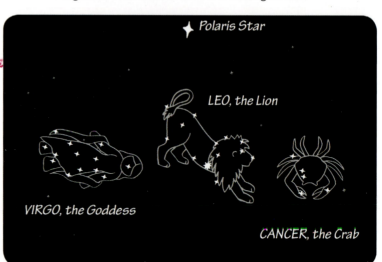

Scrambler

Unscramble the words associated with Leo the Lion.

1. NIOL
2. YRUB
3. EIFR
4. NSU
5. KCLBA
6. ULAYFLP
7. RTAEH
8. NOUBTRSB
9. GLURUES
10. YOBMALANFT

Do you see what I see? Who or what...might it be?
What teachings could be held so high...
As to be written in the night sky?

VIRGO

August 23 — September 22

VIRGO
the goddess

I am Virgo. Virgo, the Goddess.

The Goddess of righteousness and justice.

I am adaptable and industrious,

Intellectual and practical, too

I think critically and skeptically.

In my ceaseless pursuit for simple perfection

I have an insatiable urge to make improvements

Suggesting enhancements,

whether they're needed or not.

And in everything I set forth to do, I give it my all.

As I approach life with wisdom and experience

My motto is, "I Analyze!"

DID YOU KNOW?

There is an old adage to help you find the star Spica, of Virgo, in the Springtime: "Follow the arc to Arcturus (ark-tur-us) and speed onto Spica (speeka)." So, follow the curve in the handle of the Big Dipper to the first bright orange star, which is Arcturus. Then, continue the arching to the first bright blue star; this is Spica.

VIRGO, the Goddess
August 23 - September 22

The sixth of the twelve constellations, Virgo is positioned between Leo, the Lion, and Libra, the Scales.

From the earliest Babylonian times, the Grain Goddess Nidoba was considered to be the representation of Virgo.

Virgo, which can be translated to mean "self-contained," and then interpreted to mean "self-sufficient," was the Great Goddess and Mother of all things on Earth. She was a woman, an individualist, and a nurturer, the Goddess of harvest and of justice, and a caretaker of mankind.

Born under Virgo

You are said to be...

- Smart, Analytical, and Rational

But you can also be...

- Rigid, Critical, and Narrow-Minded

Colors: SILVER, WHITE
Stone: OPAL
Mode: MUTABLE
Metal: NICKEL
Body Part: STOMACH

Fill in the missing blank *-OR-* Draw in the missing symbol. (See Aspect Chart on **page 5**.)

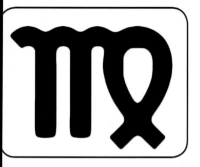

Celestial: MERCURY

Element: EARTH

Virgo represents the motto, "I ANALYZE"
   ★ To ANALYZE: to examine things diligently
   ★ To ANALYZE: to evaluate on a practical level
   ★ To ANALYZE: to be considered a reliable individual

If you are...
   ★ Alone most of the time and unable to make and keep friends
   ★ Dissatisfied with your life, with no excitement
   ★ Thinking that you will never reach your goals

Then Virgo teaches you to...
   ★ Exchange criticism for compliments
   ★ Be less restrictive with the rules you set for yourself
   ★ Express positive traits using analytical reasoning

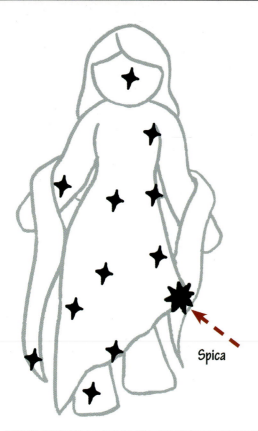

- ★ Spica may look like one star, but it's actually two stars, both larger and hotter than our sun.

- ★ Virgo is the largest constellation in the Astrological Zodiac, second largest constellation of all the constellations, after Hydra.

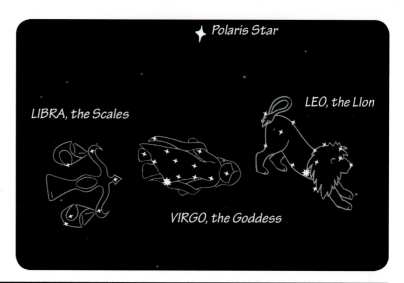

TRANSLATION

Some of the message is already decoded.
Translate the rest by using the decoder box below.

1. Virgo, the Great ᗅ ᗅ ᗅ ᗅ ᗅ ᗅ

2. Stone: ᗅ ᗅ ᗅ ᗅ

3. Body Part: ᗅ ᗅ ᗅ ᗅ ᗅ ᗅ ᗅ

4. Motto: "I ᗅ ᗅ ᗅ ᗅ ᗅ ᗅ ᗅ"

5. Element: ᗅ ᗅ ᗅ ᗅ ᗅ

6. Two stars hotter than our sun: ᗅ ᗅ ᗅ ᗅ ᗅ

7. Second ᗅ ᗅ ᗅ ᗅ ᗅ ᗅ Constellation

DECODER

ᗅ	A	ᗅ	M
ᗅ	B	ᗅ	N
ᗅ	C	ᗅ	O
ᗅ	D	ᗅ	P
ᗅ	E	ᗅ	R
ᗅ	G	ᗅ	S
ᗅ	H	ᗅ	T
ᗅ	I	ᗅ	U
ᗅ	J	ᗅ	Y
ᗅ	L	ᗅ	Z

Do you see what I see? Who or what...might it be?
What teachings could be held so high...
As to be written in the night sky?

LIBRA

September 23 — October 22

LIBRA
the scales

I am Libra. Libra, the Scales.
I seek harmony in my surroundings.
I am the moral foundation of an ideal way.
Weighing without bias, so that balance prevails
Every day I am a model of love, beauty, and grace
Deeply appreciating all things, great and small.
I am not argumentative, despite any disagreements
As a preventative, I have weighed it out fairly.
Strong willed, I accomplish my goals.
Approaching life with a regard for equality
My motto is, "I Balance!"

DID YOU KNOW?

Scales have long been associated with legal/court systems. They are referred to as "The Scales of Justice" and are meant to represent the balance of each side of an argument: fair and equal representation without bias, in one way or another.

LIBRA, the Scales
September 23 - October 22

The seventh of the twelve constellations, Libra is positioned between Virgo, the Goddess, and Scorpio, the Scorpion.

The scales are said to belong to Astrea, the Goddess of Justice, who also carried a double-edged sword. A daughter of Zeus, Astrea presided over the affairs of mortals. Though blind, she had the gift of second sight—the ability to foresee the future.

She was one of the last gods to leave Earth for the heavens. It is said that when she left, with her went the "Golden Age of Man," a time known for great happiness and ease.

Born under Libra

You are said to be...

- Charming, Generous, and Resourceful

But you can also be...

- Emotional, Argumentative, and Easily Offended

Colors: BLUE, BLACK
Stone: SAPPHIRE
Mode: CARDINAL
Metal: BRASS
Body Part: KIDNEYS and LOWER BACK

Fill in the missing blank *-OR-* Draw in the missing symbol. (See Aspect Chart on page 5.)

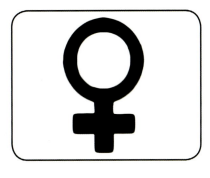

Symbol: LIBRA

Element: AIR

Libra represents the motto, "I BALANCE"
★ To BALANCE: a diplomatic way—both sides are weighed
★ To BALANCE: an idealistic way—perfect equilibrium
★ To BALANCE: a sociable ambience—remaining poised

If you are...
★ Frustrated with others and punishing yourself for it
★ Ill from situations that are only slightly irritating
★ Repeatedly finding yourself trapped in situations

Then Libra teaches you to...
★ Express positive self-worth by first pleasing yourself
★ Cultivate your inner security with spiritual strength
★ Don't have pretend feelings, gracefully back-out before getting trapped

★ Libra is the only inanimate constellation, meaning it is not animal, human, or a combination of both.

★ The youngest constellation, its stars were once the claws of Scorpio, before becoming separated and forming its own constellation.

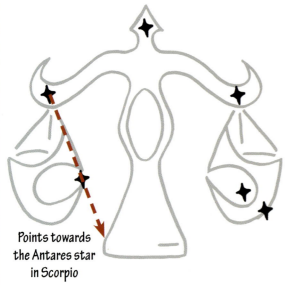

Points towards the Antares star in Scorpio

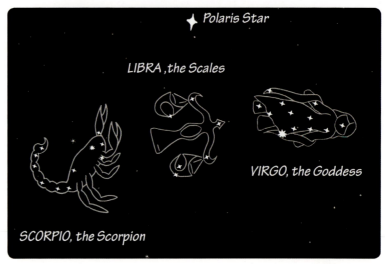

Using the words listed below, find the words associated with Libra in the puzzle. Words are horizontal, vertical and diagonal.

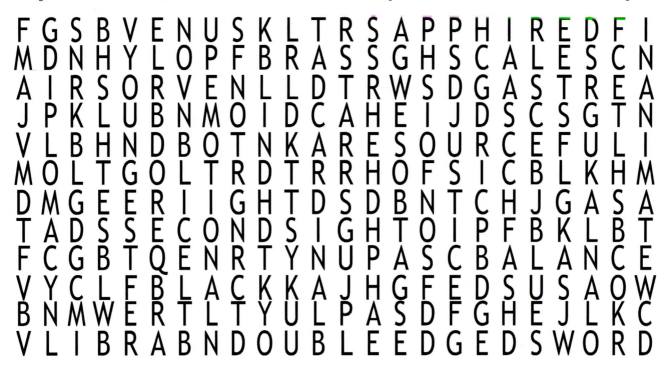

LIBRA	BRASS	YOUNGEST	ASTREA	INANIMATE	RESOURCEFUL	BLIND
SCALES	BLUE	SAPPHIRE	JUSTICE	EMOTIONAL	SECOND SIGHT	AIR
VENUS	BLACK	CARDINAL	BALANCE	DIPLOMACY	DOUBLE EDGED SWORD	

Do you see what I see? Who or what...might it be?
What teachings could be held so high...
As to be written in the night sky?

SCORPIO

55

October 23 — November 21

SCORPIO
the scorpion

I am Scorpio. Scorpio, the Scorpion.

I am a loyal and dedicated friend.

I have a curious fascination

Passionate, with emotions that run deep.

Even if I seem easygoing, I really like to be in control.

I'm not competitive, unless of course you push me.

And though my enthusiasm can be overwhelming

At the heart of it, there is an inspiring sincerity.

I am passionate and ambitious.

As I approach life with intensity

My motto is, "I Desire!"

DID YOU KNOW?

It is a myth that scorpions are only found in deserts or hotter regions. There are species that can live successfully where temperatures get cold enough to freeze. Antarctica is the only place on Earth where Scorpions cannot live.

Scorpio, the Scorpion

October 23 - November 21

The eighth of the twelve constellations, Scorpio is positioned between Libra, the Scales and Sagittarius, the Archer.

In Greek mythology, Scorpio (or Scorpius) was the known enemy of Orion the Hunter. It was Scorpius who did the bidding of the Gods and stung Orion on the foot for boasting that he was *the greatest hunter in all the Universe—better than the Gods*. Unfortunately, the scorpion sting killed Orion. However, the Gods immortalized them both and placed them in the heavens, but on opposite sides. This was to keep them from continuously fighting each other.

Born under Scorpio

You are said to be...

- Passionate, Charming, and Ambitious

But you can also be...

- Manipulative, Vengeful, and Menacing

Colors: MAROON, BLACK
Stone: HEMATITE
Mode: FIXED
Metal: PLUTONIUM
Body Part: SKIN

Fill in the missing blank *-OR-* Draw in the missing symbol. (See Aspect Chart on **page 5**.)

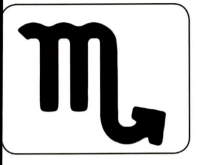  

Celestial: PLUTO

Scorpio represents the motto, "I DESIRE"
★ To DESIRE: to long for more passion and love
★ To DESIRE: to crave more excitement and thrills
★ To DESIRE: to want more intuition and insights

If you are...
★ Feeling troubled, bothered and put upon
★ Noticing or picking out the shortcomings of others
★ Suffering from self-disgust or an inferiority complex

Then Scorpio teaches you to...
★ Find what it is that you are really after - to be content
★ Change your own attitude, watching what you say
★ Forgive yourself first, so you can then forgive others

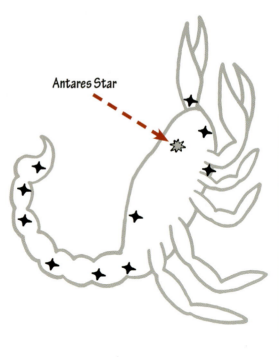

Antares Star

★ Antares is the "beating heart" of Scorpio. It is a red supergiant and the brightest star in Scorpio.

★ Currently, the accepted name for this constellation is Scorpius, even though the Zodiac name is labeled Scorpio.

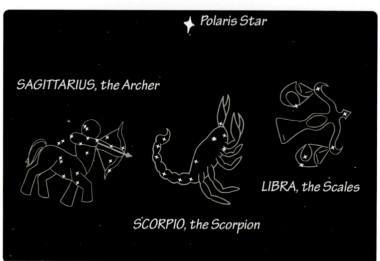

Solve the math equations. Then match the answer to the letter. Decode the puzzle revealing some of Scorpio's different aspects.

12 + 4 = ___ = A   10 - 3 = ___ = F   3 + 3 = ___ = M   9 - 5 = ___ = S

1 - 0 = ___ = B   10 + 7 = ___ = H   8 + 6 = ___ = N   8 - 5 = ___ = T

2 - 3 = ___ = C   13 + 2 = ___ = I   6 + 5 = ___ = O   12 - 2 = ___ = U

7 + 1 = ___ = D   12 + 6 = ___ = K   5 - 3 = ___ = P   10 + 9 = ___ = W

5 + 0 = ___ = E   6 + 6 = ___ = L   4 + 5 = ___ = R   12 + 1 = ___ = X

1) __ __ __ __ __ __
   6 16 9 11 11 14

2) __ __ __ __ __
   7 15 13 5 8

3) __ __ __ __ __
   2 12 10 3 11

4) __ __ __ __ __ __ __
   17 5 6 16 3 15 3 5

5) __ __ __ __ __
   19 16 3 5 9

6) __ __ __ __ __ __ __ __
   2 12 10 3 11 14 15 10 6

7) __ __ __ __ __ __
   8 5 4 15 9 5

Do you see what I see? Who or what...might it be?
What teachings could be held so high...
As to be written in the night sky?

SAGITTARIUS

November 22 — December 21

SAGITTARIUS
the archer

I am Sagittarius. Sagittarius, the Archer.
A centaur by nature, yet a man at my core
I can find wit and laughter in any situation.
Addicted to life, I treasure each and every day.
I have an overactive ambition...a free spirit
With an honest and optimistic disposition.
I am an independent idealist with a keen intellect.
I crave knowledge and I strive to know the truth.
I am forever filled with energy and enthusiasm.
As I approach life curiously
My motto is, "I See!"

DID YOU KNOW?

The Archer is actually a centaur, a creature from mythological times that is described as having the head, arms, and torso of a man and the body and legs of a horse. Most centaurs were wild, showing the truest will of raw-animal nature.

SAGITTARIUS, the Archer
November 22 - December 21

The ninth of the twelve constellations, Sagittarius is positioned between Scorpio, the Scorpion, and Capricorn, the Sea Goat.

Sagittarius is known as a centaur, meaning he was half-man and half-horse. Most centaurs were known for being savage brutes, except for Chiron. Chiron was a teacher of medicine, hunting, and archery.

One day, Chiron was accidentally wounded by a poisonous arrow. Because he was the son of the god Kronos, he did not die, but was doomed to life forever suffering from his injury. However, Zeus granted him a painless immortality as the constellation Sagittarius.

Born under Sagittarius

You are said to be...

- Unique, Casual, and Optimistic

But you can also be...

- Restless, Impulsive, and Self-Righteous

Colors: RICH PURPLE, RED
Stone: TOPAZ
Mode: MUTABLE
Metal: TIN
Body Part: HIPS and BUTT

Fill in the missing blank *-OR-* Draw in the missing symbol. (See Aspect Chart on **page 5.**)

Celestial: JUPITER

Element: FIRE

Sagittarius represents the motto, "I SEE"
- ★ To SEE: to view a positive, optimistic outcome
- ★ To SEE: to understand and uphold honesty
- ★ To SEE: to behold of others an intellectual side

If you are...
- ★ Tethered to a spot, unable to move forward
- ★ Lost and disillusioned, disappointed in a belief
- ★ Unable to confide in yourself, or find time for yourself

Then Sagittarius teaches you to...
- ★ Focus on one thing at a time, working towards a goal
- ★ Set reasonable goals to move forward with endeavors
- ★ Not be quarrelsome or exaggerate

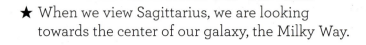

★ When we view Sagittarius, we are looking towards the center of our galaxy, the Milky Way.

★ Sagittarius contains a distinct teapot shape within its star pattern. On a clear night, the Milky Way looks like the steam coming from the spout.

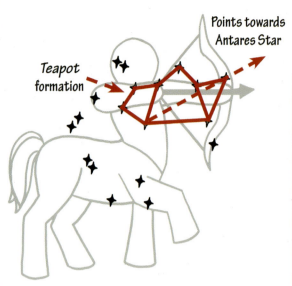

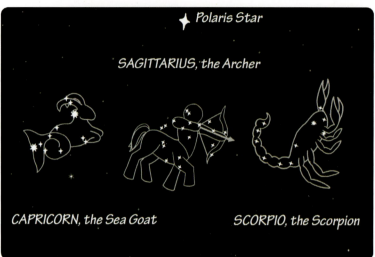

Chiron taught and trained Gods and Heroes like: _____

Answer the questions below and fill in the boxes. The answer to the question in the box above, will be revealed in the circles.

1. Body: _____ and Butt

2. Elemental Aspect

3. Became Sagittarius

4. Sagittarius, the _____

5. You can be _____ ...

6. But, also _____

7. Color: _____

8. Motto: "I _____!"

Do you see what I see? Who or what...might it be?
What teachings could be held so high...
As to be written in the night sky?

CAPRICORN

December 22 — January 19

CAPRICORN
the sea goat

I am Capricorn. Capricorn, the Sea Goat.

I am grounded in traditional values.

A faithful and loyal friend to so many

Confident and practical, not easily knocked down

Standing on a foundation of responsibility.

I can assess the worth of a situation.

Nothing stands in the way of my ambitions for success.

I am disciplined, working hard and long each day

Thinking deeply, I explore all the possibilities,

As I approach life ambitiously

My motto is, "I Use!"

DID YOU KNOW?

The Sea Goat, Capricorn, was said to have the head and front legs of a goat with the tail of a fish. The constellation is located in an area of the sky appropriately referred to as the "Water" or "Heavenly Sea."

CAPRICORN, the Sea Goat
December 22 - January 19

The tenth of the twelve constellations, Capricorn is positioned between Sagittarius, the Archer and Aquarius, the Water Bearer.

Born on the longest night of the year, legends says that Capricorn was originally a satyr, half-goat and half-man. Then one day, the Titan, Typhon, began causing havoc—trying to wipe out the Gods of Mount Olympus. The satyr jumped into the sea, trying to avoid the path of destruction that Typhon was creating.

He was forever safe now, living amongst the children of Poseidon. He was destined to remain in the sea, and thus his legs were transformed into a fish tail.

Born under Capricorn

You are said to be...

- Witty, Clever, and Tenacious

But you can also be...

- Pessimistic, Competitive, and Single-minded

Colors: BLUE, BROWN
Stone: BLACK ONYX
Mode: CARDINAL
Metal: LEAD
Body Part: KNEES and SKELETON

Fill in the missing blank **-OR-** Draw in the missing symbol. (See Aspect Chart on **page 5**.)

  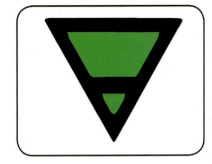

Celestial: **SATURN**

Capricorn represents the motto, "I USE"
- ★ To USE: to apply a daily practicality to life
- ★ To USE: to utilize, to make good use of disciplines
- ★ To USE: to benefit from the teachings of patience

If, you are...
- ★ Finding that others take advantage of you
- ★ Finding that people don't want to work with you
- ★ Tired of a project before it's been completed

Then Capricorn teaches you to...
- ★ Be wary of favors, to put yourself first sometimes
- ★ Work with people on their level, not above them
- ★ Pace yourself, don't overdo yourself or your schedule

★ Capricorn is the second faintest and the smallest of all the Zodiac constellations.

★ Deneb is the brightest star in Capricorn. Dabih, is the second brightest star in Capricorn, though it is actually not a star; it's a star system.

Crossword Puzzle

DOWN
1. half-man, half-goat
2. Body: _____
3. Stone: _____
5. Color: _____
8. Elemental Aspect

ACROSS
4. Mode: _____
6. Motto: "I _____"
7. Said to be _____
9. Celestial Body
10. Can be _____

Do you see what I see? Who or what...might it be?
What teachings could be held so high...
As to be written in the night sky?

AQUARIUS

January 20 — February 18

AQUARIUS
the water bearer

I am Aquarius. Aquarius, the Water Bearer.

I am an independent thinker—acting on practicality

Working best in a structured environment.

I have an inspirational ability when I focus.

Needing to make my own judgments

I am considered an unorthodox pioneer and skeptic

Unpredictable, I tend to deviate from my plans.

I am imaginative and inventive,

Treasuring an artisan's uniqueness

I approach life with originality

My motto is, "I Know!"

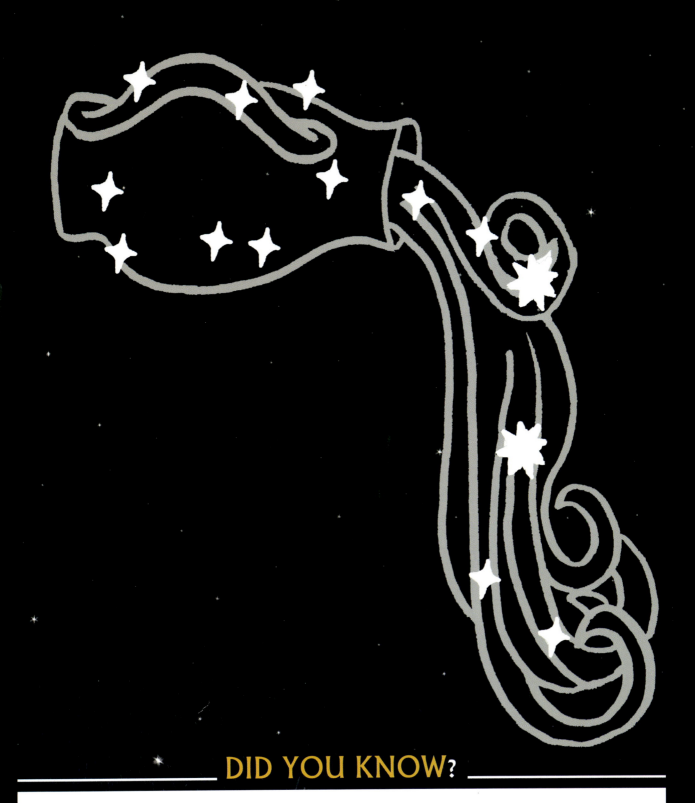

DID YOU KNOW?

Aquarius is not a Water sign, though it is often mistaken for one. It is actually an Air sign, because a person in this sign is able to separate from their emotions in order to trust their instincts.

AQUARIUS, the Water Bearer

January 20 - February 18

The eleventh of the twelve constellations, Aquarius is positioned between Capricorn, the Sea Goat and Pisces, the Fish.

Aquarius, also known as the "God of Two Streams," is said to be a youthful male. He was water borne on the back of an eagle on its way to Mount Olympus.

It is said that spilling forth from his cup is the "Age of Aquarius" (the 21st century). With this new age comes a flowing stream of new wisdom for the good of humanity. It is thought that this new age will bring with it an era where spirituality will be wholly embraced.

Born under Aquarius

You are said to be...

- Idealistic, Imaginative and Open-Minded

But you can also be...

- Thoughtless, Childish and Anti-Social

Colors: TURQUOISE, WHITE
Stone: TURQUOISE
Mode: FIXED
Metal: URANIUM
Body Part: ANKLES and CALVES

Fill in the missing blank *-OR-* Draw in the missing symbol. (See Aspect Chart on page 5.)

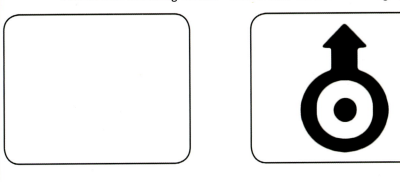

Symbol: AQUARIUS

Element: AIR

Aquarius represents the motto, "I KNOW"

★ To KNOW: to understand the importance of friendship

★ To KNOW: to recognize the importance of loyalty

★ To KNOW: to appreciate the importance of honesty

If you are...

★ Feeling secluded from others, by your own doing

★ Feeling like you miss out on bigger and better things

★ Constantly getting ill, more than you should

Then, Aquarius teaches you to...

★ Learn to accept others as they are

★ Use a positive approach to get what you want

★ Express, not repress, the feelings that eat away at you

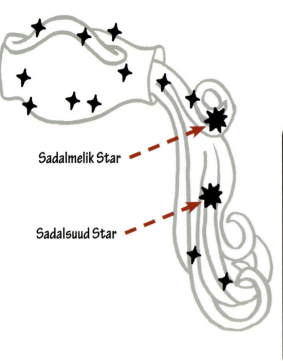

★ The Sadalsuud star is a rare class of yellow super giants. Sadalsuud has a mass six times greater than our sun.

★ The Sadalmelik star is a giant star. It has a diameter that is one hundred times bigger than our sun.

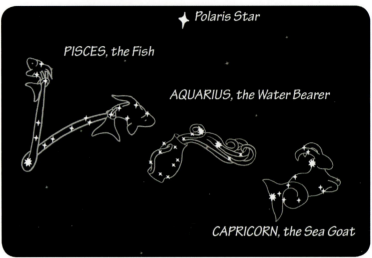

Scrambler

Unscramble the words associated with Aquarius the Water Bearer.

1. IRA

2. WKON

3. DEXFI

4. SKNELA

5. EITWH

6. NARUUS

7 & 8.

TRAWE

AERRBE

9. UINAMRU

10. IOUSQTURE

Do you see what I see? Who or what...might it be?
What teachings could be held so high...
As to be written in the night sky?

PISCES

February 19 — March 20

PISCES
the fish

We are Pisces. Pisces, the Fish.

We have an intense imagination,

a tendency to embellish.

More instinctively, than intellectually

We trust in our personal intuitions.

Reacting to life on the defensive – we are survivors.

We aren't afraid to break troublesome principles.

Being focused and strong, we overcome our weaknesses,

Then retreat into a dream world of satisfaction.

Approaching life with mysticism

Our motto is, "I Imagine!"

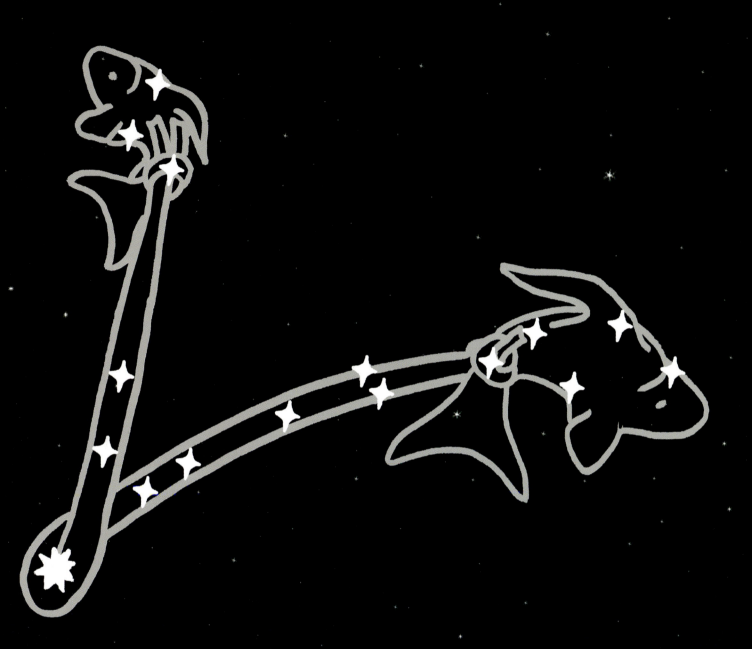

DID YOU KNOW?

The reason that the fish are heading in two different directions has a lot to do with the personality traits of a Pisces. One part of you being "caught in the current" of everything and the other part of you just wants to "swim away" from reality.

PISCES, the Fish
February 19 - March 20

The last of the twelve constellations, Pisces is positioned between Aquarius, the Water Bearer, and Aries, the Ram.

When the frightful Typhon attacked Mount Olympus, the Gods wouldn't fight him; instead they fled.

Fearing capture, the Goddess Aphrodite grabbed her son, Eros, and tied a silver cord to him so they wouldn't become separated from each other. She then asked the water nymphs to turn them into fish so they could swim to safety. They swam to the ends of the earth and beyond...into the safety of the heavens and far out of reach of Typhon, forever.

Born under Pisces

You are said to be...

- Receptive, Artistic, and Compassionate

But you can also be...

- Unforgiving, Irrational, and Unpredictable

Colors: SEA GREEN, BLUE
Stone: MOONSTONE
Mode: MUTABLE
Metal: PLATINUM
Body Part: FEET and TOES

Fill in the missing blank *-OR-* Draw in the missing symbol. (See Aspect Chart on **page 5**.)

Celestial: NEPTUNE

Element: WATER

Pisces represents the motto, "I IMAGINE"

★ To IMAGINE: to create and live in a different reality

★ To IMAGINE: to envision a reality of perfection

★ To IMAGINE: to create a reality of secrecy

If you are...

★ Feeling a strong sense of despair or loneliness

★ Causing issues and people are walking out on you

★ Finding that you seem to never have enough

Then Pisces teaches you to...

★ Change your way of thinking in your particular situation

★ Empower yourself to inspire others around you

★ Lighten up! (Sometimes we push ourselves too hard to meet our own ideals.)

★ The Alrescha star is the brightest star in Pisces and the third brightest star of all the Zodiacs.

★ *Alrescha* comes from the Arabic word meaning "the cord." The star essentially pins the ribbon which binds the two fish together in the heavens.

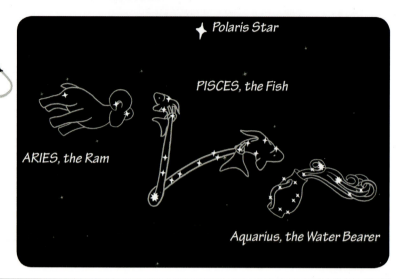

Alrescha Star

TRANSLATION

Some of the message is already decoded.
Translate the rest by using the decoder box below.

1. Color: ⛧⚸⚷ ⚕♍⚸⚸♅

2. Stone: ⚹♍⚸♅⛧⚸♍♅⚸

3. Element: ⚻⚸⚹⚸♍

4. Celestial Body: ♅⚸⚷⚹⚻♅⚸

5. Motto: "I ⚕⚹⚸⚕⚕♅⚸"

6. Metal: ⚷⚸♌⚹⚕♅⚹

7. ⚸⚹♍⚸⛧♍⚸⚸, it means "the cord"

DECODER

⚸	A	♅	N
♃	B	⚷	O
♍	C	⚺	P
♍	D	♍	R
⚸	E	⛧	S
⚕	G	⚹	T
⚿	H	⚻	U
⚕	I	⚻	W
⚹	L	♏	Y
⚹	M	♏	Z

THE THIRTEENTH ZODIAC

November 29 — December 17

OPHIUCHUS
the serpent bearer

Ophiuchus, which means serpent-bearer,
Is recognized as a man,
Wrangling a large serpent in his hands.
His one foot can be found
Just above the back of Scorpio,
And the other foot looks as though
It will be stung by Scorpio's stinger.

OPHIUCHUS, the Serpent Bearer
November 29 - December 17

As the thirteenth constellation, Ophiuchus is positioned between Scorpio, the Scorpion, and Sagittarius, the Archer.

The acknowledgment of Ophiuchus is not a new discovery. It is argued that Ophiuchus was always meant to be part of the Zodiac, as it is one of the original eighty-eight constellations.

Astrobiologists have known about this constellation since ancient times. However, it is a fairly new revolution to want to initiate this constellation into the Sun Signs, based on different theories.

There are theories that state that it couldn't be added (in the beginning) because the ancients divided the sky into twelve sections, since there were only twelve solar months. Supposedly, to have added it into the Zodiac would have meant that it would have to conform to a lunar cycle of thirteen moons instead.

This additional Zodiac is not widely accepted by many and thus difficult for many to conform to. The last change was made in roughly 2000 BCE (over 4,000 years ago), with the claws of Scorpio being broken off to form the Libra Scales and thus giving us our twelfth Astrological Zodiac.

Element: FIRE

Motto: "I DARE"

Celestial Body: MARS

Colors: GREEN, BROWN

Stone: BLOODSTONE

Mode: FIXED

Metal: TITANIUM

With Ophiuchus as part of the Astrological Zodiac the Sun Sign dates are as follows:

Aries: April 18 - May 13

Taurus: May 13 - June 21

Gemini: June 21 - July 20

Cancer: July 20 - August 10

Leo: August 10 - Sepeptember 16

Virgo: September 16 - October 30

Libra: October 30 - November 23

Scorpio: November 23 - November 29

Ophiuchus: November 29 - December 17

Sagittarius: December 17 - January 20

Capricorn: January 20 - February 19

Aquarius: February 16 - March 11

Pisces: Mar.ch 11 - April 18

IMPORTANT!

Despite whether you acknowledge Ophiuchus as an Astrological Zodiac or not, nothing really changes. Our individual personalities are based on more than just our Sun Signs. We also inherit traits from other aspects including (but not limited to) environmental impacts, family lifestyles, and our karma, too.

Answer Keys

ARIES:

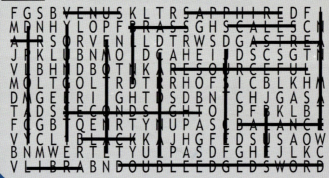

TAURUS:
1. Asterope
2. Taygeta
3. Maia
4. Celaeno
5. Electra
6. Merope
7. Alcyone

GEMINI:
1. Gemini
2. Emerald
3. Immortal
4. Castor
5. Pullox
6. Air
7. Troy

CANCER:
Down
1. Dependable
2. Ways
4. Moon
5. Silver
6. Pearl

Across
3. Crab
6. Poseidon
7. Water
9. Brave

LEO:
1. Lion
2. Ruby
3. Fire
4. Sun
5. Black
6. Playful
7. Heart
8. Stubborn
9. Regulus
10. Flamboyant

VIRGO:
1. Goddess
2. Opal
3. Stomach
4. Analyze
5. Earth
6. Spica
7. Largest

LIBRA:

SCORPIO:
1. Maroon
2. Fixed
3. Pluto
4. Hematite
5. Water
6. Plutonium
7. Desire

SAGITTARIUS:
1. Hips
2. Fire
3. Chiron
4. Archer
5. Unique
6. Impulsive
7. Red
8. See

CAPRICORN:
Down
1. Satyr
2. Knees
3. Black Onyx
5. Blue
8. Earth

Across
4. Cardinal
6. Use
7. Clever
9. Saturn
10. Witty

AQUARIUS:
1. Air
2. Know
3. Fixed
4. Ankles
5. White
6. Uranus
7 & 8. Water Bearer
9. Uranium
10. Turquoise

PISCES:
1. Sea Green
2. Moonstone
3. Water
4. Neptune
5. Imagine
6. Platinum
7. Alrescha